ANXIETY RELIEF
JOURNAL FOR TEENS

ANXIETY *Relief* JOURNAL *for* TEENS

Guided Exercises to Help You Manage
Anxiety, Ease Stress, and Find Calm

Brandi Matz, MSW, LCSW

ILLUSTRATED BY FRANCES MACLEOD

ROCKRIDGE
PRESS

Interior and Cover Designer: Elizabeth Zuhl
Art Producer: Hannah Dickerson
Editor: Sean Newcott
Production Editor: Melissa Edeburn

Illustration © 2021 Frances MacLeod

ISBN: 978-1-63807-500-4
R0

This journal belongs to:

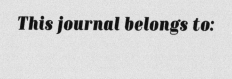

"A journey of a thousand miles begins with a single step."

—LAO TZU

Contents

Introduction

Welcome to the *Anxiety Relief Journal for Teens*. I'm Brandi Matz, a therapist specializing in anxiety and the author of *Cultivating Calm: An Anxiety Journal*. It is important to start by acknowledging that everyone has some level of anxiety. Anxiety is a normal human emotion, just like happiness or sadness. However, sometimes when a person has too much anxiety, it can be overwhelming. It can prevent you from doing things that you want to do or even impact your daily life. Over the past 20 years, I have worked with many teens dealing with excessive anxiety and made it my mission to find the most effective strategies and coping skills specific to teens and young adults. Your teenage years are all about figuring out who you are and who you want to be, making it a perfect time to focus on self-awareness and self-care. If you would like to learn ways to manage your anxiety and feel better about yourself, journaling is a great place to begin.

Anxiety is the most common struggle among Americans today, especially teens. This is important for you to know so that you recognize you are not alone in your worries. Nobody likes to feel anxiety, and people experience it in different ways. Sometimes, it is felt physically, such as a racing heart, sweating, splotchy skin, headaches, feeling hot, or stomachaches. Other times, anxiety can be felt mentally, such as overthinking and racing thoughts. Regardless of how it manifests for you, anxiety can affect your ability to be social; it can impact school performance or interactions with friends. Excessive worrying and overthinking can lead to sleep issues and also affect your happiness and overall quality of life. It can be debilitating and even scary sometimes. The good news is that anxiety is manageable.

Journaling can be a powerful method to provoke change: It is an effective therapeutic tool that helps you process your feelings, better understand where your anxiety comes from, and prioritize your goals. Processing your thoughts through writing can help you express your emotions in a healthy way and reduce your overall stress. The intention of this journal is to help you discover the best ways to lower and manage your anxiety so you can begin to feel content, confident, and relaxed.

How to Use This Journal

In each of this journal's three sections, you will find prompts, practices, and quotes. The prompts will ask you to explore and write about your thoughts and feelings. The practices will give you examples of coping skills and strategies to try in stressful situations to reduce anxiety. And the quotes are meant to inspire you as you set out to manage your anxiety and embrace more happiness.

You can use this journal in whatever way works best for you, but you will benefit most if you move through it section by section and work through it consistently, whether that's setting aside a quiet time each day to journal. You can also use it in times of high stress as a coping tool.

The first section of the book, Hello, Anxiety, focuses on learning about anxiety and yourself. Through self-reflection, you will uncover how you view yourself and your anxiety and how these views have impacted your life. In this section, you will lay the groundwork for where you want to go, who you want to be, and what you want to achieve.

In the second section, Let It Go, you will identify your fears and triggers—as well as how your body responds to stress—and how to take control of your anxiety instead of letting it control you. You will learn to recognize unhealthy thought patterns, how they can affect your behavior, and how to change those patterns. This section will also explore how these core beliefs can support, rather than prevent, your goals.

The third and final section of the book, Calm, Cool, and Relaxed, will teach mindfulness strategies—or the act of being present in the moment—for managing anxiety and establishing healthy routines. You'll learn techniques for meditation, breathing, and visualization in order to practice self-care and track and maintain your progress.

This journal is designed to help you learn more about yourself and your anxiety and how you can achieve your personal goals, but it is not meant to replace professional help. If you are experiencing excessive anxiety that impacts your daily life or are having thoughts of suicide or self-harm, it is very important to tell a trusted adult and seek professional help through a therapist or psychiatrist. There is no shame in asking for help. Investing in yourself is the most important thing you can do to live a happy, successful life. I am so pleased you are willing to learn and grow, and I am honored that you have chosen this journal as one of your tools. Best of luck in your journey. You're worth it.

PART ONE

Hello, Anxiety

To be happy and content is a choice, though sometimes making that choice can be challenging if you're feeling anxious. Today, know that you *are* capable of making a choice to change your life by using this journal to help guide you where you want to go.

This section will lay the foundation for change, and the first step is to get to know yourself and practice self-awareness: Identify your fears, how you view yourself, and the role anxiety plays in your life. One of the all-time best ways to become self-aware is journaling because it allows you to take a step back to better process your feelings, beliefs, and actions. Self-reflection through journaling helps you examine the "why" of a feeling or situation more objectively, which in turn helps you make choices to feel happier or more content.

In the pages ahead, you will explore what is considered "normal" anxiety versus overwhelming anxiety, and how you uniquely experience anxiety yourself. People get anxious about different things. Some people have social anxiety, while others feel anxiety about academic performance or what-if scenarios. It's important to identify what triggers your anxiety so that when it happens, you can take a deep breath, understand what you're feeling, manage the feelings, and take control of the anxiety before it takes control of you. As you journal about what makes you feel anxious and how anxiety can impact you, don't be surprised if you learn some new things about yourself that are true but weren't necessarily obvious before. If that process makes you feel a little vulnerable, don't be afraid of it! Your vulnerability is what helps you grow the most. You got this!

"When we own the story, we can write a brave new ending."

—BRENÉ BROWN

≈ Anxiety is uncomfortable, but it is a normal human emotion that anyone can experience, just like feeling happy, sad, or angry. Though no one enjoys feeling anxious, sometimes it can feel more than uncomfortable and rather overwhelming.

Describe what you think "normal" anxiety should feel like.

_____

_____

_____

_____

_____

How do you experience anxiety?

_____

_____

_____

_____

_____

In order to change something in your life, it's important to know where you want to end up. In order to achieve the goals you have set for yourself, sometimes it is helpful to think of a person you admire, specifically their admirable qualities. Once you know what it is you want, it's easier to figure out a way to get there.

Everyone experiences anxiety, but how do you know if what you are experiencing is "normal"? Some anxiety can actually be beneficial, such as when you have a test coming up and the anxiety you feel about getting a good grade motivates you to study harder. But other times, anxiety can come from irrational causes and disrupt your daily life.

Write about the times when you have experienced anxiety in a "normal" way versus an irrational way.

_____

_____

_____

_____

_____

_____

_____

_____

_____

_____

_____

_____

Based on your reflections, do you think your anxiety is "normal" or irrational?

_____

_____

_____

_____

_____

_____

_____

_____

_____

_____

_____

_____

_____

_____

_____

When your body perceives a threat, it alerts your sympathetic nervous system and prepares your body to fight or flee the situation. This is an evolutionary adaptation of survival that keeps you safe in dangerous situations. People who suffer from anxiety, however, often have an overactive nervous system, which tricks your body into thinking that situations are threatening even when they're not. Exercise can be a wonderful way to calm your nervous system either when anxiety is trying to take control or as a way to prevent anxiety from cropping up.

Identify ways you can exercise each day to keep your body feeling calm and in control.

_____

_____

_____

_____

_____

_____

_____

_____

≋ How do you experience anxiety physically?

Write about how your body feels—from your head to your toes—when your anxiety is triggered.

_____

_____

_____

_____

_____

_____

_____

_____

_____

_____

_____

_____

_____

What kinds of events, people, or feelings trigger your anxiety? Is your anxiety triggered by classmates, social media, parents, school?

Write down your specific triggers to better understand where they come from.

_____

_____

_____

_____

_____

_____

_____

_____

_____

_____

_____

_____

Now that you have identified your anxiety triggers, keep a log each day for a week in order to track when you feel anxiety and what triggered it. It's helpful to look back at your log and see if there are any patterns. For example, is there a time of day when you typically feel anxious? Knowing your patterns will help you anticipate times when you are likely to be anxious and prepare for them by having coping strategies in place.

	ANXIETY AND TRIGGER	ANXIETY AND TRIGGER	ANXIETY AND TRIGGER
MONDAY			
TUESDAY			
WEDNESDAY			
THURSDAY			
FRIDAY			
SATURDAY			
SUNDAY			

"Bravery is being the
only one who knows
you're afraid."

—FRANKLIN P. JONES

Now that you've logged how, when, and why you feel anxious, you may be able to identify some patterns.

Do you notice any patterns in your anxiety log?

_____

_____

_____

_____

Does your anxiety feel worse at a certain time of day?

_____

_____

_____

_____

Is your anxiety related to hunger or sleep?

_____

_____

_____

_____

Reflect on what you learned from your anxiety log.

_____

_____

_____

_____

_____

_____

_____

_____

_____

_____

_____

_____

_____

Knowing your own unique needs and how to meet them is part of the self-reflection and self-care process. Identify what your physical and emotional needs are. (For example: *I need eight hours of sleep to feel well rested; I need to exercise to relax my body; I need to journal to understand my feelings; I need to practice meditation to calm my mind.*)

_____

_____

_____

_____

_____

_____

_____

_____

_____

_____

_____

Now that you are aware of both your physical and emotional needs, make a schedule for the week—you can cover everything from school to social events to family time. Each day, note a specific time to ensure those physical and emotional needs are met.

MONDAY			
TUESDAY			
WEDNESDAY			
THURSDAY			
FRIDAY			
SATURDAY			
SUNDAY			

The best person to depend on to take care of your physical and mental health is you. But you can be hard on yourself sometimes, which can damage your self-esteem and self-confidence.

Find a picture of yourself when you were young and write a letter to that child telling them all of the things you love about them.

_____

_____

_____

_____

_____

_____

_____

_____

_____

_____

Read this letter often to remind yourself that you are responsible for that child's well-being and happiness and should be as kind to yourself as possible.

≥ Think of the people in your life with whom you are close.

Make a list of those who trust and support you.

_____

_____

_____

_____

_____

_____

What is it about these people that makes you
trust them?

_____

_____

_____

_____

_____

_____

≋ Think about the list of people you trust the most.

What qualities or traits do you share with them?

_____

_____

_____

_____

_____

_____

_____

What qualities or traits do you wish to develop for
yourself?

_____

_____

_____

_____

_____

_____

_____

What has the last year of your life been like? Write about the positive things that have happened, as well as the lessons you learned from any challenging experiences.

_____

_____

_____

_____

_____

_____

_____

_____

_____

_____

_____

_____

Reflect on how your fears and anxiety have limited you.

Have there been things that you have not done or participated in due to your fears?

_____

_____

_____

_____

_____

_____

_____

_____

_____

_____

_____

_____

_____

What do you wish you did differently?

_____

_____

_____

_____

_____

_____

_____

_____

_____

_____

_____

_____

_____

_____

_____

"*Getting knocked
down in life is a given.
Getting up and moving
forward is a choice.*"

—ZIG ZIGLAR

What are the three most important things that you wish to accomplish this year? Why do you wish to accomplish these things?

Now that you have identified the three things you wish to accomplish this year, make a realistic plan to achieve them. Be as specific as possible.

What obstacles could you encounter?

_____

_____

_____

_____

_____

_____

_____

_____

_____

_____

_____

_____

How will you avoid those obstacles?

_____

_____

_____

_____

_____

_____

_____

How will you stay motivated to accomplish your goals?

_____

_____

_____

_____

_____

_____

_____

What do you spend the most time worrying about? Why does this worry you so much?

_____

_____

_____

_____

_____

_____

_____

_____

_____

_____

_____

_____

_____

Cognitive distortions are ways that your mind tricks you into seeing things not exactly as they are. Sometimes, this happens when you overgeneralize by saying things like "always" and "never" or by only seeing the negative in situations. Some examples of this kind of thinking are "*I never make friends*" or "*I always let people down*." If you struggle with cognitive distortions, the easiest way to correct it is to acknowledge that you are doing it in the first place. Write about any cognitive distortions you recognize in yourself.

Anxiety can be genetic, but it can also be learned. Sometimes, if a parent or guardian is overly anxious, you might learn that being anxious is normal. Think about your family.

Do you notice anxiety or depression in any family members? In what ways?

_____

_____

_____

_____

_____

How has their behavior impacted how you feel, behave, or act?

_____

_____

_____

_____

_____

_____

"You are the sky. Everything else— it's just weather."

—PEMA CHÖDRÖN

≈ Many people begin to experience anxiety early in life.

When is the earliest time in your life that you remember experiencing feelings of anxiety?

_____

_____

_____

_____

_____

_____

_____

_____

_____

_____

_____

_____

_____

What kinds of things made you anxious?

_____

_____

_____

_____

_____

How did you handle your anxiety at that time?

_____

_____

_____

_____

_____

_____

_____

_____

_____

Lots of people use and enjoy social media, but even if you're scrolling through photos of people having fun or doing interesting things, it can take a toll on you if you're automatically comparing yourself to those people.

How do you actually feel about social media?

_____

_____

_____

_____

_____

_____

_____

_____

_____

_____

_____

Have you ever been negatively impacted by social media? Describe when, how, and the circumstances surrounding the memory. (For example: Seeing friends together when you weren't invited; Comparing your body to other bodies.)

_____

_____

_____

_____

_____

_____

_____

_____

_____

_____

_____

_____

"The man who moves a mountain begins by carrying away small stones."

—CONFUCIUS

≋ Although it may not be obvious in the moment, constantly scrolling through social media can be detrimental to your mood and sense of self-worth. Track the time you spend on social media for one week and how the images and words you see make you feel. You may be surprised at how much time you are actually scrolling!

MONDAY

TUESDAY

WEDNESDAY

THURSDAY

FRIDAY

SATURDAY

SUNDAY

Change can be scary, but just by using this journal, you are acknowledging some desire for change. Be proud of yourself for the work you are doing to meet your personal goals!

What has held you back from change so far?

_____

_____

_____

What's different now?

_____

_____

_____

How can you make sure that you continue to work through these challenges?

_____

_____

_____

_____

"There are plenty of difficult obstacles in your path. Don't allow yourself to become one of them."

—RALPH MARSTON

There is a lesson to be learned with every situation, no matter how well or poorly it went.

What is the biggest challenge that you have faced in your life so far?

Describe what happened and the outcome.

_____

_____

_____

_____

_____

_____

_____

_____

_____

_____

_____

_____

What lessons did you learn from this challenge?

_____

_____

_____

_____

_____

_____

_____

_____

_____

_____

_____

_____

_____

_____

_____

With anxiety, it can be difficult to focus on positivity because so much energy is reflexively put into thinking about the worst-case scenarios. To combat the negative and focus on the positive, each day—either right after you wake up or right before you go to bed—write down three to five things that you are grateful for. Do this at the same time each day. Practicing gratitude is a wonderful way to stand up to anxiety.

≷ Laughter is good for your soul.

When was the last time you laughed? What was the last thing that made you laugh? Write about the details of the memory.

_____

_____

_____

_____

_____

_____

Who are the people in your life that make you laugh the most? Make a list and describe why you think each person listed is responsible for injecting so much laughter into your life.

_____

_____

_____

_____

_____

≽ Introverts get energy from being alone, while extroverts get energy from being around people. It's also possible for someone to be both a little introverted and a little extroverted. It may be that there are times when you like to be around people, but too many people can feel exhausting or that, after being around people, you need to recharge by spending some time alone.

Where do you fall on the introvert and extrovert continuum?

_____

_____

_____

_____

_____

_____

_____

_____

_____

_____

What are some ways that you can recharge?

_____

_____

_____

_____

_____

_____

What are some ways that you can be social?

_____

_____

_____

_____

_____

_____

_____

Some people talk freely about their feelings and their anxieties, while others are more private and keep their feelings to themselves.

Do you think it's beneficial to talk to trusted friends about your anxious feelings? Why?

_____

_____

_____

_____

_____

_____

_____

_____

_____

_____

_____

_____

In this journal, you'll learn specific coping skills for managing anxiety, but one simple thing you can start doing right now is breath control. When you learn to control your breathing, you will be able to slow your heart rate and more easily control your anxiety. Each day, set aside time to sit quietly and focus on your breathing.

1. Place one hand on your chest and the other on your belly.

2. Focus on bringing air slowly into your belly—not your chest—holding to a count of four, then slowly exhaling.

3. Try to only focus on your breathing, allowing any thoughts that enter your mind to pass by.

The food you eat can impact your mood and, depending on its ingredients, can even contribute to your anxiety. To determine if you're accidentally feeding your anxiety, track what you eat for a week below.

	BREAKFAST	LUNCH	DINNER
MONDAY			
TUESDAY			
WEDNESDAY			
THURSDAY			
FRIDAY			
SATURDAY			
SUNDAY			

Do you eat a lot of sugar?

_____

Do you consume a lot of caffeine?

_____

Are you eating mostly whole foods, or mostly processed foods?

_____

Now that you have tracked your diet, try to identify any changes you can make to avoid feeding your anxiety.

Can you cut back on coffee and drink more water?

_____

Could you eat less fast food and eat more fresh foods, like

_____

Make a list of foods that you can cut back on or eliminate and foods you can replace them with. You can also enhance your diet by adding foods that have been shown to help reduce anxiety, such as almonds and spinach, which are high in magnesium.

_____

_____

_____

_____

_____

_____

_____

Healthy sleep patterns are very important for managing anxiety, but most people who struggle with anxiety also struggle with sleep. Below, reflect on your sleep patterns.

Do you have trouble falling asleep?

_____

Do you have trouble staying asleep?

_____

Is it hard to wake up?

_____

Do you often have bad dreams?

_____

Have you always had trouble sleeping, or is this problem new?

_____

Creating a sleep routine can be very effective when trying to develop a healthy sleep cycle. Here are some things that you can try out either before or at bedtime to get better and more restful sleep:

Take a warm bath containing two cups of Epsom salt prior to bed.

Drink a warm, decaffeinated bedtime tea, such as chamomile.

Turn off your phone, laptop, and tablet an hour before you want to sleep.

Read a book; it can be something of interest, or even intentionally uninteresting.

Write a gratitude list.

Listen to a guided sleep meditation as you fall asleep.

Whatever bedtime routine speaks to you, try it for a few weeks and make changes to your approach as needed until you find the best strategy for you. Your body may take some time to adjust, so don't give up if it doesn't work right away.

In this section, you have focused on self-reflection, learned more about yourself and your needs, and set goals for your future. Self-reflection is a practice you can perform every day to achieve your goals and your full potential. Set aside time each day or each week to check in with yourself.

When you check in with yourself, ask:

How am I feeling?

_____

_____

What have I done toward reaching my goals?

_____

_____

Am I following my self-care routine?

_____

_____

What could I have improved on this week?

_____

_____

What did I do well?

_____

_____

How do I feel about my efforts so far?

_____

_____

What is my focus going to be this week?

_____

_____

What am I grateful for?

_____

_____

PART TWO

Let It Go

You've done an awesome job so far! You've learned what your needs are and how to take good care of yourself. You've explored your thoughts and feelings about anxiety and pinpointed where it stems from. You've set realistic goals and developed a plan to achieve them. Now that you've successfully spent some time self-reflecting, you're ready to shift your focus to change—the kind that benefits you and helps you feel more calm, more relaxed, and less anxious.

Your mind can lead you to think negatively about situations that may not be as negative as you believe. This section will tackle cognitive distortions, identifying how they come up and how to change your thought patterns. You'll also learn how to change the what-if questions that anxiety can feed into what-is statements that focus on comforting truths rather than worst-case scenarios. If your mind gets stuck and automatically thinks negative thoughts, you'll learn ways to change this pattern and start having more positive, supportive thoughts. Identifying your negative thoughts is not always easy; sometimes, it can even be scary to let go of your negative thoughts because it feels like they serve a purpose. Remember, you are strong and capable of change. It takes time and practice to alter your thought patterns, so be patient with yourself. The best goal to set for yourself is to make each week better than the last and take baby steps until you reach your bigger goals.

"You don't have to control your thoughts. You just have to stop letting them control you."

–DAN MILLMAN

⇛ *Filtering* is a type of cognitive distortion in which you tend to focus on a singular negative aspect of an event or situation despite there being many positive aspects to the event or situation. Have you ever found yourself doing this? If so, write down some examples of situations in which you filtered out the good and focused on the bad.

_____

_____

_____

_____

_____

_____

_____

_____

_____

_____

_____

_____

≷ Identifying your cognitive distortions can be difficult, but it is a crucial step in beginning to change them for the better. List what makes you feel anxious and reflect on what you think and how you feel about each event, person, or thing that you listed. (For example: *I get anxious about giving a presentation. I think that everyone will be able to tell how nervous I am.*)

_____

_____

_____

_____

_____

_____

_____

_____

_____

_____

_____

_____

_____

≳ Take each anxiety that you listed on page 59 and challenge each one.

ANXIETY	CHALLENGE
Nervous about presentation	*What is the worst thing that could happen if people can tell I'm nervous? They are probably nervous, too. Nothing bad will happen to me from feeling nervous. I will be okay. I know strategies to lower my anxiety, and I will use them.*

"A positive attitude gives you power over your circumstances instead of your circumstances having power over you."

–JOYCE MEYER

⇉ *Core beliefs* are beliefs that you have adopted, typically in early childhood, as the result of a negative experience. Core beliefs transform into what you subconsciously tell yourself day-to-day and prevent you from doing the things you'd like to do.

Think about some of your core beliefs. (For example: *I am unlikable because, in kindergarten, a friend told me I couldn't sit with them at lunch because no one liked me.*)

Write down your most powerful core belief.

_____

_____

_____

_____

What are three things you could do to challenge this belief?

_____

_____

_____

_____

_____

_____

62

What do you think will happen when you do
these things?

_____

_____

_____

_____

_____

_____

What actually happened when you challenged
this belief?

_____

_____

_____

_____

_____

_____

_____

_____

⇌ Find a quiet spot and close your eyes. Think about something that you have anxiety about. Imagine doing that thing. Do you feel afraid? How do you physically feel? To help lower your anxiety, try this breathing technique.

1. Exhale completely through your mouth.

2. Slowly inhale through your nose to the count of 4, hold that breath for a count of 7, then exhale through your mouth to a count of 8.

3. Repeat this breathing technique as needed until you no longer associate that specific thing with anxiety but instead with relaxation.

How do you feel, act, and behave when you are anxious? Are you aware that you are acting this way in the moment?

_____

_____

_____

_____

_____

_____

_____

_____

_____

_____

_____

_____

_____

When a person experiences anxiety, their body usually has a physical reaction. Sometimes, they feel hot, their heart may race, or they feel short of breath. Below, identify all of the ways your body tells you that you are anxious. Look over your list and think about which physical sensation always happens first. Circle that symptom.

Now that you know what your first sign of anxiety is, imagine it is an alarm going off to tell you that more anxiety is on its way. Though this may seem scary, it's actually a great warning tool that will give you enough time to slow down or even reverse your anxiety symptom. One really effective way to do this is to take a slow, deep breath, focusing on filling your belly with air. It can be helpful to imagine that you are filling a balloon in your belly. This breathing technique will slow your heart rate down and keep your anxious feelings from increasing.

≋ Even though anxiety and stress are felt in the body, sometimes you can miss the signs your body is giving you because you are so focused on your stressful thoughts. Throughout the day, take a few minutes to do a body scan and release any tension you are holding.

1. Find a comfortable spot.

2. Close your eyes and focus on your breathing, slowly filling your belly with air and then slowly exhaling.

3. Bring your awareness to your feet and mentally do a scan of how your feet feel, imagining any tension or tightness leaving your feet.

4. Move your focus to your ankles and calves. Imagine the tension leaving these areas.

5. Continue to move upward through your body, releasing tension as you go, until you reach the top of your head.

6. This is a great way to mentally and physically reset throughout your day.

Self-defeating behaviors are a very common way that you may be sabotaging yourself without even realizing it. Self-defeating behaviors are any thoughts or actions that prevent you from reaching your goals. Some examples of self-defeating behaviors include perfectionism, avoidance, comparing yourself to others, overspending, self-criticism, and neglecting self-care. It's important to identify the ways in which you actively self-sabotage so you can avoid doing it moving forward. Write down all the ways you practice self-defeating behaviors that prevent you from reaching your goals.

_____

_____

_____

_____

_____

_____

_____

_____

_____

_____

Now that you have identified your self-defeating behaviors, use the following table to replace each negative behavior with one that will promote and encourage a positive mindset while working toward your goals.

SELF-DEFEATING BEHAVIOR	POSITIVE CHANGE
Overspending	*Withdraw $30 each week and only spend what I budget for.*

⇉ Your thoughts are not facts, and it's important to recognize the difference. When your thoughts feed strong or complicated emotions, they can make you feel like they must be true. To practice separating facts from feelings, take a look at the following four statements. Circle the statements that are facts and underline those that are opinions.

1. I am not attractive.

2. I am in 12th grade.

3. I am not a good person.

4. I failed my driving test.

What you tell yourself really impacts how you feel about yourself, and often those thoughts will inform whether or not you reach your goals. What are some of the thoughts that you tell yourself are facts but are really just opinions?

Because you've been experiencing anxiety, chances are you have developed a habit of negative thinking. Know that if this is true of you, it's not your fault! But any habit takes effort and practice to change, and recording your thoughts is an effective way to start changing that habit. Use this thought record to note your negative thoughts, process your thoughts and feelings, and work through how to change them for the better.

WHAT HAPPENED?	
AUTOMATIC THOUGHT	
FEELINGS	
NEGATIVE THOUGHT VS. TRUTH	
ALTERNATIVE THOUGHT	

"We acquire the strength we have overcome."

–RALPH WALDO EMERSON

Everyone has two voices in their head: a supportive voice that gives you encouragement and love and a critical voice that tells you what you need to do better or improve on. Both of these voices are important to have; however, sometimes the voice of the inner critic is louder than it needs to be.

Think about your supportive voice and your inner critic. Are they balanced? Or is one voice louder?

_____

_____

_____

_____

_____

Do you need to make some changes to those voices— their volume, what they say, or how often they say it?

_____

_____

_____

_____

_____

No one is perfect. Everyone is wonderful at heart, and everyone makes mistakes. Think of four of the people you are closest with in your life. Make a list of their names and write about their strengths and weaknesses. Write about why you love and accept them despite their faults.

Think about the compassion you feel for the important people in your life that you know aren't perfect— because no one is—but whom you still love deeply. To really change your thought patterns, start by recognizing that you owe it to yourself to show yourself love, forgiveness, and compassion. Write about the ways that you can love yourself more despite your faults.

_____

_____

_____

_____

_____

_____

_____

_____

_____

_____

_____

_____

≩ Sometimes, to build an anxiety support network, it helps to talk to friends and family ahead of time and let them know that they are on your list of trusted people.

Who are the people you are closest to?

_____

_____

_____

If you are feeling anxious, can you turn to these people?

_____

_____

_____

How can you tell them what you need when you are feeling anxious?

_____

_____

_____

_____

Take a moment to ask those on your trusted list if it's okay that you call or come to them when you're feeling anxious and need support. Together, you can decide what would be most helpful for you during those times. Use the space below to identify your top three supportive people, as well as any ways they can help you when you are feeling anxious.

_____

_____

_____

_____

_____

_____

_____

_____

_____

_____

_____

_____

When faced with something scary or challenging, a common defense mechanism is to think of the worst-case scenario. This kind of thinking will only increase your anxiety and encourage avoidance.

What is something you experienced recently that made you anxious?

_____

_____

_____

In the space below, write about the experience.

_____

_____

_____

_____

_____

_____

_____

_____

What were you thinking about?

_____

_____

_____

_____

How did it make you feel?

_____

_____

_____

_____

What was the result?

_____

_____

_____

_____

⇒ Using the example you wrote about on page 80, describe the worst thing that could've happened in that scenario.

How likely is that scenario?

_____

_____

_____

_____

_____

Will it matter in a year?

_____

_____

_____

_____

_____

_____

Is this worst-case scenario an actual fact? What
evidence supports that the scenario will happen?

_____

_____

_____

_____

_____

_____

If you change your perspective, what is the *best* thing
that could happen?

_____

_____

_____

_____

_____

_____

When you're changing your thought patterns, you may find it difficult to treat yourself with kindness and love. One way to ease into this practice is to imagine that a friend is standing by your side when you're facing a tricky situation. What advice and words of encouragement would you offer your friend if they were attempting something difficult? Write them down here and know that you can say them to yourself the next time you need some support.

≥ Positive thinking and having something enjoyable to look forward to are important parts of overall happiness. Even small pleasures like taking a bath or meeting a friend for coffee can spark feelings of joy. Do at least one thing that will bring you joy each day for the next seven days. To make sure that you reward yourself with this practice, make a schedule of what you will do each day.

MONDAY

TUESDAY

WEDNESDAY

THURSDAY

FRIDAY

SATURDAY

SUNDAY

It is common to avoid things or situations that cause discomfort. One way to tackle your fears is to face them gradually while pairing the experience with relaxation exercises. Here are some examples of situations that can cause anxiety and situations that feel more comfortable.

FEARFUL

Attending a party.
Giving a presentation.
Going on a date.

COMFORTING

Having lunch with a small group of friends.
Making a phone call.
Seeing a movie at the theater.

Write down one of your most fearful situations, then write down three less fearful situations related to that. Rank the situations from 1 to 4, with 1 being the least fearful and 4 being the most fearful.

_____

_____

_____

_____

_____

1. While breathing slowly and deeply through your belly and envisioning a positive outcome, imagine yourself in what you ranked as your least fearful situation.

2. If possible, try to actually do the item you have listed. It's okay to feel some anxiety, but you can control it with breathing techniques.

3. Move through the list as you feel more and more comfortable with acting out each situation. (If you're working with a therapist, it may be helpful to do this exercise with their help.)

"If you don't like something, change it. If you can't change it, change your attitude."

—MAYA ANGELOU

≷ Social anxiety, a symptom of which is feeling insecure and self-conscious when you are around others, is the most common form of anxiety in teens.

Do you ever feel self-conscious in a group?

_____

_____

_____

How has social anxiety impacted you and your choices?

_____

_____

_____

_____

_____

_____

_____

_____

_____

≋ Imagine your life without anxiety.

How do you think an anxiety-free life would look and feel?

_____

_____

_____

_____

_____

_____

_____

_____

_____

_____

_____

_____

_____

If you didn't have excessive anxiety, how might your life be different?

_____

_____

_____

_____

_____

_____

_____

_____

_____

Would you make different choices?

_____

_____

_____

When you work to replace negative thoughts with positive thoughts, it's important that the positive thoughts are also realistic and believable. Look at the example in the chart below, then practice your own negative thought replacement.

NEGATIVE	POSITIVE
I'm so awkward. Everyone is staring at me.	*Just because I feel awkward doesn't mean anyone can tell that's how I feel.*

To achieve a quick fix or short-term benefit, some people develop unhealthy coping strategies, like drinking alcohol, abusing drugs, oversleeping, overeating, or withdrawing socially. Make a list of any unhealthy strategies you've developed to cope with your anxiety.

_____

_____

_____

_____

_____

_____

_____

_____

_____

_____

_____

_____

Although some unhealthy coping strategies can provide a sense of instant relief, it's important to know that they don't really help you in the long term. In fact, sometimes there are negative consequences, such as with oversleeping, which can make you sluggish, miss out on events, or avoid essential responsibilities. What negative consequences have you experienced from your unhealthy coping strategies?

_____

_____

_____

_____

_____

_____

_____

_____

_____

_____

_____

Exercise, meditation, healthy eating, proper sleep habits, breathing exercises, journaling, and open communication are all examples of self-care and healthy coping strategies. Make a list of some healthy coping strategies you could try. For each strategy you list, write what you think the positive outcome of it could be.

_____

_____

_____

_____

_____

_____

_____

_____

_____

_____

_____

_____

_____

Actively practicing gratitude is a form of self-care that helps keep you in a positive mindset. When you identify one or a few things that you are grateful for each day, it can help you focus on what is good in your life. This week, think about what you're grateful for and log it on the following chart.

MONDAY	
TUESDAY	
WEDNESDAY	
THURSDAY	
FRIDAY	
SATURDAY	
SUNDAY	

Gratitude has been shown to spark positive feelings about oneself. Think about who you are grateful for these days. Write a letter of gratitude to someone who has done something for which they deserved gratitude but never received it, or write a letter to someone who conducts themself in a way that you are grateful for.

Dear _____

_____

_____

_____

_____

_____

_____

_____

_____

Sharing your feelings of gratitude with someone can boost your mood and encourage positive thinking. Feel free to send or share your letter with the person you have written it for to let them know why you are grateful for them.

⇒ The ABC Model of behavior is a helpful tool to analyze an event in your life and the thought process you experienced in response.

A stands for the activating event.

B is for your beliefs about that event.

C is for the consequences of that belief.

Use the chart below to process your experience.

ACTIVATING EVENT	BELIEFS	CONSEQUENCES
My boyfriend broke up with me.	*Irrational:* I am unlovable. *Rational:* I am able to open myself up to other people who will be a better romantic fit for me.	*Negative:* Feeling lonely and sad. *Positive:* Feeling happy to be able to spend more time with my friends.

What is something for which you need to forgive yourself? Write yourself a letter of forgiveness and allow
yourself to release any feelings of guilt or shame and
embrace feelings of compassion and relief.

Think of a time when you agreed to something that you didn't want to do.

What did you agree to do?

_____

_____

_____

_____

_____

Why didn't you say no?

_____

_____

_____

_____

_____

_____

_____

How would you like to handle the situation differently in the future?

_____

_____

_____

_____

_____

_____

_____

_____

_____

_____

_____

_____

_____

_____

If you were given three wishes, what would you wish for and why?

Liking and loving yourself are concepts that are uncomfortable to a lot of people, but they are very important in any journey to a balanced life and a healthy sense of self-esteem. What do you like about yourself? If you're having trouble answering that question, sometimes it helps to ask yourself why someone would enjoy being your friend.

Make a list of nice things people have said to you—either recently or throughout your life—and continue to add to it as the days go on.

Describe a time when you felt truly content and at ease.

What made you so content?

_____

_____

_____

_____

_____

_____

How can you replicate that sense of ease and
contentment in the future?.

_____

_____

_____

_____

_____

_____

What is a promise that you would like to make to yourself?

_____

_____

_____

_____

_____

_____

_____

_____

"We cannot become what we need to be by remaining what we are."

—MAX DE PREE

PART THREE

Calm, Cool, and Relaxed

You've come a long way. So far, you have spent time getting to know yourself, how you think about anxiety, what your triggers are, and where those triggers come from. You've set personal goals for yourself, identified how automatic negative thoughts have held you back, and learned how to positively adjust your thinking. Now it's time to focus on moving forward and establishing healthy habits so you can reach and maintain your goals.

This next section will focus on mindfulness techniques, stress management, stress reduction, self-love, and acceptance. Being mindful means being super attuned to your thoughts and feelings in the present moment; this allows you to experience the moment for exactly what it is instead of worrying about what may or may not happen later. Some mindfulness practices include meditation, grounding yourself, and breathing exercises. I encourage you to approach this section with an open mind and willingness to adopt new habits that will support your ideal self. (If it's helpful, you can look back to part 2 as a reminder of what you thought your life would be like if you didn't experience excessive anxiety.) In part 3, you will discover how great things really can look and feel by getting your anxiety under control and making peace with it. You are totally ready for, and capable of, standing up to anxiety and making your true desires and needs heard. Remember that you didn't become anxious overnight, so you shouldn't expect your anxiety to go away overnight. Simply making a choice to move forward and using the skills you have learned will make a world of difference. You've got this!

"Our life is shaped by our mind; we become what we think."

—BUDDHA

Many people experience racing thoughts when dealing with their anxiety. When you begin to feel this happening, ask yourself: "What am I feeling right now?" In fact, think about your day today. Did anything make you anxious? What were you feeling in that moment? Write down whatever comes to your mind. Do not worry about what you write or how you write it—just write! Keep writing until you feel you have nothing else to say.

Read the goals that you set for yourself on page 106. Rewrite them here. Circle the goals you have already accomplished. Then, on the following lines, write about what you are doing to accomplish your remaining goals. This will serve as a chance to check in with yourself and a reminder of where your focus needs to be.

_____

_____

_____

_____

_____

_____

_____

_____

_____

_____

_____

_____

Write about three things that made you feel happy today: a friend you hung out with, a movie you saw, nice weather, a new dish you cooked.

≋ Take a walk! If you're able, turn your phone off and go outside, paying special attention to the sounds, sights, and smells of your environment. Stay focused on what you're experiencing around you. When you finish your walk and return home, write down what you saw, heard, and smelled and how it all made you feel.

_____

_____

_____

_____

_____

_____

_____

_____

_____

_____

_____

_____

≋ Start your day off right!

What are you looking forward to today?

_____

_____

_____

_____

How will you be productive today?

_____

_____

_____

_____

How will you practice self-care today?

_____

_____

_____

_____

"Nothing can bring you peace but yourself."

—RALPH WALDO EMERSON

≋ Take some time to reflect on your day before you
go to bed.

What was the best part of your day?

_____

_____

_____

_____

What will you do differently tomorrow?

_____

_____

_____

_____

What were you grateful for today?

_____

_____

_____

_____

Sometimes, a "to-do list" can be a source of stress. Pick one thing that you need to do and set a timer for 10 minutes (or however much time you can allow). Turn off any unnecessary devices and remove any distractions from your environment. Simply focus on this one task until the timer goes off and see how productive it felt.

When anxiety begins to rise, it's important to stay grounded and in the moment. One way to pull yourself back to the present moment is to engage your five senses. Are you feeling anxious right now? If so, write down the following:

Five things you can see.

_____

_____

_____

_____

_____

Four things you can touch.

_____

_____

_____

_____

Three things you can hear.

_____

_____

_____

Two things you can smell.

_____

_____

One thing you can taste.

_____

Although it's entertaining and is a convenient way to stay connected, social media can be very distracting, and it can even be an underlying trigger for anxiety. Try logging off your social media accounts for a day. (If that feels too challenging, you can start with logging off for one hour and increase the amount of time day-by-day.) It may also help to delete the social media apps from your phone to avoid the temptation to check! (It will take more effort to download them again and log back in.) Write down how it feels to take a break from social media and whether it lowers your anxiety or gives you more time to check in with yourself and practice self-care.

_____

_____

_____

_____

_____

_____

_____

_____

"*If you want to conquer the anxiety of life, live in the moment, live in the breath.*"

—AMIT RAY

≥ Okay, so you took a social media break. How did it go?

Was it difficult?

_____

_____

_____

_____

_____

_____

Did you notice any changes in your mood?

_____

_____

_____

_____

_____

_____

Do you think it would get easier to take a break if you did it more often?

_____

_____

_____

_____

_____

_____

What positive outcomes could you enjoy if you spent less time on social media?

_____

_____

_____

_____

_____

_____

Everyone has negative experiences at one time or another, but how you choose to perceive those experiences makes the difference between being stuck in a feeling and growing from a feeling. Think about a negative experience you had recently. Instead of focusing on why it happened, write about what it taught you.

As noted on page 64, 4-7-8 Breathing is a breathing technique that slows your heart rate and helps relax your body. Practice this technique whenever you feel anxious.

Slowly inhale through your nose to the count of 4.

Hold that breath for a count of 7.

Exhale through your mouth to a count of 8.

Repeat these steps until you feel your whole body relax.

Being mindful is all about being in the moment. Think about a time when you felt you were truly *in the moment*. Write about it below, noting as many sensations, thoughts, and feelings as you can.

_____

_____

_____

_____

_____

_____

_____

_____

_____

_____

_____

_____

Self-care is vital to being mindful and feeling balanced. Make a list of five self-care practices you would like to start doing—or doing more of. (**For example:** *Drinking more water, exercising, taking a bath, organizing personal space, daily meditation.*)

1. _____

2. _____

3. _____

4. _____

5. _____

When anxiety or panic begins, your brain activates the amygdala, which is the area that experiences emotions, particularly fear and danger. Imagine that part of your brain lighting up when you feel anxious, while the rest of your brain (what is considered to be the more logical part) goes to sleep. When you're feeling anxious, your job is to wake up your entire brain in order to take energy away from the amygdala, thereby telling your brain, "There's no danger here! We're okay."

Here are some effective ways to tell your amygdala to release its grip on your energy.

Hold ice cubes in your hands.

Sing.

Listen to your favorite music.

Take a shower.

Dance.

Everyone has thoughts that are unpleasant and unwanted. When you notice that you are having these thoughts, close your eyes and visualize a big, red stop sign. In response to those unwanted thoughts, say the word "Stop" in your mind. Keep visualizing the red stop sign until the thought is successfully interrupted and leaves your mind.

There are many different ways to care for yourself: Socially, emotionally, financially, spiritually, and personally. To help you clarify your overall self-care goals, identify three ways you can care for yourself in each of the following categories.

Social:

_____

_____

_____

_____

_____

Emotional:

_____

_____

_____

_____

_____

Financial:

_____

_____

_____

_____

Spiritual:

_____

_____

_____

_____

_____

Personal:

_____

_____

_____

_____

_____

What is something you do—say, dancing, cooking, reading, or swimming—that always improves your mood? Describe how that activity has made you feel.

What does your perfect day look like from beginning to end? Write it down and be as specific as possible. Can you incorporate any of these things into your day today?

Most people dealing with anxiety hold tension in their bodies. One way to relieve this tension and melt away stress is to do an exercise called *progressive relaxation*. This technique involves focusing on a specific muscle group, tensing then relaxing the muscles, and repeating the exercise in another area, moving through one muscle group at a time.

1. Find a comfortable spot to sit or lie down.

2. Take a slow, deep breath, and then let it out.

3. Start with the muscles in your forehead, tensing them tightly and holding for 10 to 15 seconds.

4. Release the muscles and breathe out slowly.

5. Move your attention down to your jaw muscles and repeat steps 3 and 4—tensing, holding, and then releasing the muscles.

6. Continue from your head down your entire body. At the end of the exercise, your body should feel completely relaxed.

Healthy sleep habits are usually difficult to maintain if you are feeling anxious. In the space below, reflect on how you feel about sleep and your relationship to it when you're feeling anxious. What do you experience when you're trying to fall asleep? What do you need to do, or change, in order to get more restful sleep?

Did you know that magnesium supports more than 300 biochemical reactions in your body? Magnesium is a nutrient that helps keep you calm and balanced, in addition to keeping your immune system healthy, your heartbeat steady, your bones strong, and much more. When you are stressed or anxious, your body tends to use up your stored magnesium, which means there is less magnesium available to support your body's other needs. One way to replenish your body's magnesium levels is to take a bath with two cups of Epsom salt and soak for 20 minutes. Epsom salt, which is a compound of magnesium sulfate, will be safely absorbed through your skin when it's added to a warm bath. This is a great thing to do before bed especially, as it will help your body relax for sleep.

What are three things rooted in love and support that you want to tell yourself every day?

Sometimes, anxiety isn't all bad. Write about the ways anxiety has actually helped you—perhaps by motivating you or encouraging you to check in with yourself more. What have you learned about yourself by dealing with anxiety?

_____

_____

_____

_____

_____

_____

_____

_____

_____

_____

_____

_____

_____

What are the accomplishments in which you take the most pride?

_____

_____

_____

_____

_____

_____

_____

_____

_____

_____

_____

_____

_____

_____

Letting go of intrusive thoughts can be difficult. One trick for achieving this is to pick a color—it could be your favorite color—look around your environment, and identify everything that is your chosen color. Let's say you pick the color blue. While sitting in your room, you might identify a blue lamp, a blue stapler, a blue pen, a blue T-shirt . . . the list goes on and on! Before you know it, your mind is laser focused on the task of finding blue things instead of focusing on the intrusive thoughts.

What does it mean to you to have healthy habits? Outline a daily routine that incorporates healthy habits into your life. Some ideas could be to wake up 20 minutes earlier and meditate, make a to-do list for the day, go running or take a walk, prep your food for the day, or take a bath before bed.

Are you a good listener? Sometimes, when people feel anxious, they tend to get distracted by thinking about what they want to contribute to a conversation instead of really hearing what the other person is saying.

Write about a time when someone was being a good listener with you.

_____

_____

_____

_____

_____

What made you feel that they were listening to and understanding you?

_____

_____

_____

_____

_____

_____

In your next conversation, be aware of these things and try your best to be an active listener.

Adding stretching to your daily routine is not only good for your body but also allows you to pause and connect with your body each day. Set aside a few minutes at the start of each day to stretch your body a little bit. Take your time and feel your body release any tension it is holding.

⇒ Here is a meditation for stress release.

1. Find a quiet and comfortable spot to sit down and close your eyes.

2. Imagine yourself walking up a steep, grassy hill, taking your time with each step.

3. Feel the warm breeze in your hair and smell the fresh scent of the grass.

4. With each step you take up the hill, imagine that you are releasing some of the anxiety you are feeling.

5. When you reach the top of the hill, focus on your breathing by taking a slow, deep breath and holding it for five seconds.

6. When you exhale, picture all of the stress leaving your body and evaporating into the air.

It is common to feel worried about the things that you cannot control. When this happens, it can be helpful to write out what is and what is not within your control about a particular situation. If you identify that the majority of your worries are about circumstances that are not within your control, it can be easier to let them go.

THINGS WITHIN MY CONTROL	THINGS *NOT* WITHIN MY CONTROL

When you're having negative thoughts, ask yourself, "How are they helping me?" If they are not actually helping you, imagine them blowing away like a puff of smoke.

"You can't stop the waves, but you can learn to surf."

–JON KABAT-ZINN

What is one thing you can do each morning to make your day better? What is one thing you can avoid each day to make room for self-care and compassion?

You can't always help worrying, but you can plan it. Hear me out! Basically, instead of feeling anxious that worry will creep up in moments you least expect it or when you really need to focus, set aside a block of time each day to acknowledge your worries. When you can have a moment to yourself, set a timer for about 10 minutes and allow yourself to worry about anything you want or need to during that time. When the timer goes off, it's time to stop worrying until the next scheduled worry time, either later in the day or the next day. It may seem strange at first, but it may comfort you to have set times to observe your worry without feeling like your whole day is overtaken by it. This method can help you compartmentalize your worries until you are ready to let them go and live free of anxiety.

Write a letter to your past self. Forgive yourself for the times when you were self-critical. With your new mindfulness lessons in mind, give yourself advice about moving forward with self-care and compassion, and share with your past self all the amazing things that you will ultimately accomplish.

"Just when the caterpillar thought the world was ending, he turned into a butterfly."

—PROVERB

Parting Words

Making the choice to work on yourself is something that you should be proud of. This is a perfect time to decide who you want to be and make it happen. You are in control of your life! Take some time to look back through this journal and see how far you've come and celebrate the progress you have made. Things won't be perfect all the time—life rarely is, and perfection is not the goal. Accepting that you are always in a state of growth is a sign of emotional maturity. When in doubt, remember that each day is an opportunity for a fresh start.

Revisit this book's practices as you move forward. Be proud of yourself and what you have accomplished. Remember, no one gets through life alone, and there is no shame in asking for help. So, if at any time you feel overwhelmed or that you could use some help, ask for it. Ask a parent, a family member, a trusted adult, a friend, or a professional. And just as you will build your circle of trusted friends and family for support, you, too, can be a person that someone else can lean on in times of need.

You've come so far in your mindful journey to overcoming anxiety, and at the same time, it has just begun! Keep moving forward. I know you are going to accomplish great things.

Resources

To find a therapist in your area or online:

BetterHelp.com: A resource for online counseling. Offers virtual and text messaging options.

BrandiMatz.com: This is my personal website. I offer online therapy, and you can contact me through the site.

PsychologyToday.com: Psychology Today's website offers listings of licensed therapists in your area, and you can view each therapist's specialization, cost, experience, etc.

SAMHSA.gov: Substance Abuse and Mental Health Services Administration (SAMHSA) is a government program that provides information and resources, including how to find help.

TalkSpace.com: Another resource for online counseling. Also offers virtual and text messaging options.

Websites

ADAA.org: The Anxiety & Depression Association of America provides a lot of useful articles, research, and information about anxiety. It is also another resource to find a therapist.

HelpGuide.org: HelpGuide is a nonprofit organization with a mission to provide valuable content regarding mental health.

NationalSocialAnxietyCenter.com: The National Social Anxiety Center is a great resource if you are struggling with social anxiety and are looking for information and tips.

Psychiatry.org: The American Psychiatric Association is an organization for medical professionals as well as families and individuals looking for information about mental health and mental illness.

WebMD.com: WebMD can be useful for looking up symptoms and ways to manage your anxiety.

Books

The Anxiety and Phobia Workbook by Edmund J. Bourne, PhD

Little Ways to Keep Calm and Carry On: Twenty Lessons for Managing Worry, Anxiety, and Fear by Mark A. Reinecke, PhD

References

Brandt, Andrea, PhD, MFT. "3 Steps to Treat Your Anxiety Using CBT." *Psychology Today.* Accessed March 10, 2021. PsychologyToday.com/us/blog/mindful-anger/201906/3 -steps-treat-your-anxiety-using-cbt.

Gibson, Cameron, RCC. "How to Overcome Social Anxiety in High School." WikiHow. Accessed March 12, 2021. WikiHow .com/Overcome-Social-Anxiety-in-High-School.

Martin, Ben, PsyD. "In-Depth: Cognitive Behavioral Therapy." PsychCentral. Accessed March 12, 2021. PsychCentral.com /lib/in-depth-cognitive -behavioral-therapy#1.

McLeod, Saul. "Cognitive Behavioral Therapy." Simply Psychology. Accessed March 10, 2021. SimplyPsychology.org/cognitive-therapy.html.

Pietrangelo, Ann. "9 CBT Techniques for Better Mental Health." Healthline. Accessed March 12, 2021. Healthline.com/health/cbt-techniques.

Princing, McKenna. "These At-Home Cognitive Behavioral Therapy Tips Can Help Ease Your Anxieties." Right as Rain by UW Medicine. Accessed March 12, 2021. RightAsRain.uwmedicine.org/mind/stress/these-home -cognitive-behavioral-therapy-tips-can-help-ease -your-anxieties.

Acknowledgments

It is my honor to have been given the opportunity to work with so many amazing young adults over my career. They make me laugh and teach me something new every time; they have helped me grow both personally and professionally. For the first time in my professional life, I have two adolescent children. People assume because I work with teens that I know what I'm doing; however, I can assure you that we all learn as we go. I only hope that my kids know how loved they are and will always feel safe coming to me for guidance. A big thank-you to my daughter Grace for her time and effort contributing ideas and quotes to this journal. Thank you to all of the kids and families who have trusted me and taught me more than I ever could have learned in school.

About the Author

 **Brandi Matz**, MSW, LCSW, author of *Cultivating Calm: An Anxiety Journal*, has spent the last 20 years working in a variety of settings, including inpatient, residential, and outpatient hospitals; public, private, and alternative high schools; and private practice. She resides in Connecticut with her husband and two children and has a full-time private practice specializing in anxiety. She provides online therapy to individuals who want help with anxiety. Learn more at www.BrandiMatz.com.

CPSIA information can be obtained
at www.ICGtesting.com
Printed in the USA
LVHW071906020721
691782LV00009B/55